Vidal Espinosa, MBA and Arturo Soler

# HELP!
## I want to be a real estate investor
### *What Do I Do?*

## Disclaimer

The author and publisher of this book have used their best efforts when preparing this book and any accompanying materials. Throughout the book, the author and publisher make no representation or warranties with respect to the accuracy, applicability, fitness or completeness of the contents.

They disclaim any warranties (expressed or implied), merchantability or fitness for any particular purpose. The author and publisher shall in no event be held liable for any loss or other damages, including, but not limited to, special, incidental, consequential, or other damages.

As always, the advice of a competent legal, tax, accounting or other professional should be sought. The author and publisher do not warrant the performance, effectiveness or applicability of any sites listed in this book. All links are for information purposes only and are not warranted for content, accuracy or any other implied or explicit purpose.

This book contents material protected under International and Federal Copyright Laws and Treaties. Any unauthorized reprint or use of this material is prohibited.

# HELP!
# I want to be a real estate investor
# *What Do I Do?*

Giving peace of mind on how to save taxes while maximizing profit on a real estate investment.

by
Vidal Espinosa, MBA
and
Arturo Soler, Investor

Vidal Espinosa, MBA and Arturo Soler

ISBN-13: 978-1537456485
Arthur Kathleen Publishing
Copyright 2016

## Dedications

*To all of my supporters, partner, and family who have given me the freedom to go after my dreams – V.E.A.*

*To my wife and children who inspire me to continue to undertake new challenges.*

*To Vidal Espinosa for believing in my vision.*

*To my entire team at ARSO Real Estate Premier who have supported me unconditionally. – A.S.*

# Table of Contents

Introduction ........................................................................................... 9

How do I get started? .......................................................................... 10

Can I invest if I live and reside in another country? ............................ 15

Should I put my investment into a business entity? ........................... 18

What kind of business entity is best for me? ....................................... 19

Which is the best business entity for Real Estate Investors? ............. 29

Who should I have on my "Power Team"? .......................................... 31

What is my first big decision? .............................................................. 32

How do I find a property? ..................................................................... 36

Are there any pitfalls I should look out for? ......................................... 38

Is this property a good investment? ..................................................... 40

Can I get the cash to purchase my real estate investment? ............... 42

I have my property, now what? ............................................................ 45

How can I (legally) pay less taxes on my profits? ............................... 46

What if I have losses on my real estate investment? ......................... 51

Are there tax incentives for Real Estate Investments? ...................... 53

About the Authors ................................................................................ 56

About Invictus Advisors ....................................................................... 58

About ARSO Real Estate Premier ...................................................... 59

# Introduction

**"As long as you have more cash flowing in than flowing out, your investment is a good investment."** - **Robert Kiyosaki**

If your intentions are to buy real estate to generate more cash, and if you want to have the cash now rather than years from now, then listen up. There is more to investing in real estate than just getting rich quick. It is about protecting yourself and your family, reducing the amount of taxes that you will have to pay Uncle Sam, and selecting the best property so you can maximize your profits.

While some might lead you to believe that there is a simple answer that works for everyone, this simply isn't the case. We have built this book to help you simplify the process of figuring out how to get started. Of course this is not intended to be an all-encompassing "how-to" on real estate investing but merely an overview of some of the tax and legal implications you should address before you start your first real estate investment.

## How do I get started?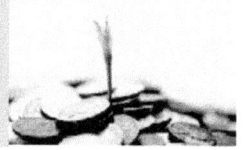

Believe it or not, getting started is all in your head. You have to be prepared mentally before you head into the tough world of Real Estate Investing. There are huge firms that like to put the smaller guys out of business but as long as you are committed, focused and determined, you will find a property that will fit your needs. Despite abundant advertisements claiming that real estate investing is an easy path to wealth, it is in fact a challenging business requiring expertise, planning and focus.

Though it may be relatively simple to enjoy short-lived profits, developing a viable real estate investing business that can last for the long-term requires additional skill and effort. Whether focusing on apartment buildings or commercial property, highly effective real estate investors share these 10 essential habits.

**Tips for success**
- A good attitude
- Self-belief
- Ability to grow
- Focus
- Enthusiasm

### 1. Treat Investments as Businesses

It is important for real estate investors to approach their real estate activities as a business in order to establish, and achieve, short and long-term goals. A business plan allows real estate investors to not only identify objectives, but also determine a viable course of action towards their attainment. A business plan also allows investors to visualize the big picture, which helps maintain focus on the goals rather than on any minor setback. Real estate investing can be complicated and demanding, and a solid plan can keep investors and management organized and on task.

2. **Know Your Markets**

   Effective real estate investors acquire an in-depth knowledge of their selected market(s). The more an investor understands a particular market, the more qualified he or she will be to make sound business decisions. Keeping abreast of current trends, including any changes in consumer spending habits, mortgage rates and the unemployment rate, to name a few, enables savvy real estate investors to acknowledge current conditions and plan for the future. Being familiar with specific markets allows investors to predict when trends are going to change, creating potentially beneficial opportunities for the prepared investor.

3. **Maintain High Ethical Standards**

   Realtors are bound to act according to a code of ethics and standards of practice policy, and real estate agents are held to each state's real estate commission rules and standards. Real estate investors, however, unless they are associated with membership-based organizations, are not usually required to maintain a particular degree of ethics in their business practices, as long as they operate within the boundaries of the law. Even though it would be easy to take advantage of this situation, most successful real estate investors, and especially those who remain in the business for the long haul, maintain high ethical standards. Since real estate investing involves actively working with people, an investor's reputation is likely to be far reaching. In the case of an investor lacking in ethics, the consequences can be damaging. Effective real estate investors know it is better to conduct fair business, rather than seeing what they can get away with.

4. **Develop a Focus or Niche**

   Because there are so many ways to invest in real estate, it is important for investors to develop a focus in order to gain the depth of knowledge essential to becoming successful. This involves learning everything about a certain type of investment - whether it is wholesaling or commercial real estate - and becoming confident in that area. Taking the time to develop this level of understanding is integral to the long-term success of the investor. Once a particular market is mastered, the investor can move on to additional areas using the same in-depth approach. Savvy investors know that it is better to do one thing well than five things poorly.

5. **Strive to be Good Customer Service Representatives**

   Referrals generate a sizable portion of a real estate investor's business, so it is critical that investors treat others with respect. This includes business partners, associates, clients, renters and anyone with whom the investor has a business relationship. Effective real estate investors are good customer service representatives by paying attention to detail, listening and responding to complaints and concerns, and representing their business in a positive and professional manner.

6. **Stay Educated**

   As with any business, it is imperative to stay up to date with the laws, regulations, terminology and trends that form the basis of the real estate investor's business. Keeping current does require additional work, but it can be viewed as an investment in the future of the business. Investors who fall behind risk not only losing momentum in their businesses, but may also face legal ramifications if laws are ignored or broken. When it pertains to the law, ignorance is no excuse. Successful real estate investors take the time and make the effort to stay educated, adapting to any regulatory changes or economic trends.

7. **Understand the Risks**

   Those choosing to invest in the stock or futures markets are inundated with myriad warnings regarding the inherent risks involved in investing. Numerous agencies require disclaimers to warn potential market participants about the possibility of loss of capital. While much of this is legalese, it has made it clear to people that investing in the stock or futures markets is risky; meaning one can lose a lot of money. Investors understand the risks associated with the business and adjust their businesses to reduce any risks.

8. **Invest in a Reputable Accountant**

   Taxes comprise a significant portion of a real estate investor's yearly expenses. Understanding current tax laws can be complicated and take time away from the business at hand. Sharp real estate investors retain the services of a qualified, reputable accountant to handle the business's books. The costs associated with the accountant can be negligible when compared to the savings a professional can bring to the business.

9. **Find Help When They Need It**

   Real estate investing is complicated and requires a great deal of expertise to engage profitably in the business. Learning the business and the legal procedures is challenging to someone attempting to do things on their own. Effective real estate investors often attribute part of their success to others - whether a mentor, lawyer, accountant or supportive friend. Rather than risk time and money solving a difficult problem on their own, successful real estate investors know it is worth the additional costs (in terms of money and ego) to find help when they need it and embrace other peoples' expertise.

10. **Build a Network**

    A network can provide important support and create opportunities for a new or experienced real estate investor. This group of associates can be comprised of a well-chosen mentor, business partners, clients or a non-profit organization whose interest is in real estate. A network allows investors to challenge and support one another, and can aid significantly in advancing one's career through shared knowledge and new opportunities. Because much of real estate investing relies on experiential-based learning, rather than on reading a book, for instance, savvy real estate investors understand the importance of building a network.

These 10 habits are important, but most people don't realize that finding help and building a network are two essential steps that need to be done before you start on the path of real estate investing. You need to develop you "Power Team" to help you get through your investments.

> Five Critical Skills you need to be an investor:
> - Be persistent and willing to preserve
> - Keep current and flexible
> - Be positive and confident
> - Be organized and stay focused
> - Be dedicated and patient

## Can I invest if I live and reside in another country?

Buying property in the U.S. may seem easier than in many other countries. The real estate markets are open and there is generally no ban on foreign investment in property (personal or corporate). But beware - U.S. real estate markets can be complicated, depending upon where the property is located. Each state has its own rules and regulations for property transfer-- that means 50 different sets of rules! It pays to be well-educated at the start, particularly as the purchase relates to U.S. taxes for expats. Tax implications are often ignored in the buying process but certainly should be on your radar.

While you are encouraged to contact an experienced real estate agent and an expert tax accountant, we have compiled four tips to help you begin the process:

### Planning to borrow to buy?

According to U.S. Census results, 70 percent of homes in the U.S. are mortgaged. Mortgages are also a large chunk the banking industry. It will take a lot of documentation to obtain a mortgage from a U.S. bank, but the mortgage rates are low and the interest paid on the loan is tax deductible on your U.S. taxes, if you have any taxable income, or if you should choose to rent. There are additional benefits to mortgaging property with a U.S. bank: most banks

Here are a few questions as a foreigner should know before buying real estate in America:

a. How are you planning to use it?
b. Where are you planning to buy?
c. What are the purchasing rules?
d. What are the legal issues?
e. Who can help?
f. How are you paying?
g. Are you ready to pay taxes?
h. Are you prepared for the process?

require the proper transfer of title; property insurance; and escrow accounts that pay property taxes and insurance. This saves you the hassle of dealing with these individually. Additionally, your mortgage provider will provide you with an annual statement for tax purposes detailing all aspects of your transactions.

You will pay property taxes in the U.S. The U.S. tax system is separate for property taxes. In many states, you will pay higher taxes if you are not a permanent resident, so make sure you look into your tax rate as a non-U.S. resident. Don't assume the taxes paid by the seller will be the same as yours. If the property is a rental property - the tax will reduce your taxable income on the property for U.S. tax purposes.

## Will you have to file U.S. taxes?

Maybe, maybe not! This is a complicated question, but here are some general thoughts. Nonresident aliens are taxed on U.S. investment income and their U.S. trade or business income (Sec. 871); so depending upon the purpose of your purchase, you may not be required to file income tax returns, i.e. if it is a pied-a-terre. If you plan to rent, there is possibility of filing as a business or a trade, which allows all deductions and losses from the activity to be claimed on your U.S. taxes. Otherwise, the real estate income is subject to the flat 30 percent withholding tax levied on a gross basis. So you may want to consider renting the property for a portion of the year, as it could defer some of the holding costs of your property without adding taxes.

## Should I use a corporation to buy property?

We would encourage you to do so but it depends upon your purpose for purchasing. A foreign corporation that earns investment income in the United States or conducts a U.S. trade or business must file a U.S. tax return. The rules governing U.S. taxation of a foreign corporation's income parallels those for nonresident aliens; but keep in mind that in addition to the regular tax, foreign corporations are also subject to the alternative minimum tax, accumulated earnings tax, and personal holding company tax. The main advantage of using a corporation is liability protection.

## How long can I spend in the U.S.?

If you are planning to buy a home in the U.S. and spend time there, this issue really affects your taxes. Remember, the rules for residency in the US are different for paying taxes than for any other purpose. The U.S. has a two pronged question that determines residency - a physical presence test and a lawful residency test. If you pass either - you are a resident of the U.S. for tax purposes. The physical presence test can get complicated, but it boils down to the days you spend on U.S. soil.

> **FOR EXAMPLE:** *If you stay in the United States for 31 or more days during the current calendar year and a total of 183 or more days during the current and the two preceding tax years, you have presence. (each day in the current year is weighted one, each day in the first preceding year is weighted one-third, and each day in the second preceding year is weighted one-sixth.)*

Having presence in the U.S. means you will be ineligible for tax deductions and exclusions given to those having a primary residence overseas. These deductions and exclusions are critical to reducing U.S. taxes for expats looking to avoid double taxation (being taxed on income in both their home and host country). So if you plan to reside primarily overseas, it is important to carefully calculate the number of days you spend in the U.S. to protect those tax credits! Note- this is a different Physical Presence Test to the one used to gauge your expat tax status.

Buying property in the U.S. can be a great experience, and afford you the best of both worlds -- living abroad while maintaining a property in your home country. It simply takes you and your "Power Team" to the properly plan, understand and consider all factors to ensure it's the right financial choice for you.

## Should I put my investment into a business entity?

If you have assets, a home or a salary of more than $100,000 the simple answer is "YES" but truthfully, it depends.

The best way to really find out is to talk to a tax professional but here is a rough guide to determine if you should consider opening a Corporation or an LLC:

Do you:
- ☐ have a home or personal assets?
- ☐ need tax flexibility?
- ☐ need additional deductions on your taxes?
- ☐ think your business will ever be liable for over what your current business policy limits are?
- ☐ have high personal income?

Are you planning on:
- ☐ looking for investment capital?
- ☐ going public or issuing stocks?
- ☐ transferring ownership?
- ☐ selling or passing your business to your children or other individuals?
- ☐ growing your business to double the size it is now?

If you have:
- ✓ **More than 50%** - Definitely talk to an accountant to see if opening a Corporation or LLC is right for you!
- ✓ **Less than 50%** - You are probably not quite ready to open a business entity but you soon will be!

## What kind of business entity is best for me?

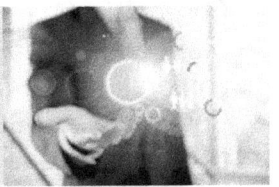

Selecting a business entity is a decision that should not be taken lightly. Many places that claim to "incorporate fast", incorporate online" or "low-cost incorporate" are probably not the best and most professional way to go. There are many steps and forms needed to make sure that you are thoroughly protected. Additionally, professional guidance is needed to explain the corporate reporting to the State, complicated tax consequences and strategy, and the correct use of the corporation.

Here are the four business entity types (that the IRS recognizes) and the Pros and Cons for each:

### Sole Proprietorship

A Sole Proprietorship (also known as a "DBA", "Doing Business As", or a "Fictitious Business Name") is a business that is not separate from its owner, merely a different name that the business owner operates under. The owner is **personally liable** for the company and its debt; all income is added on the owner(s) personal tax returns (pass-through taxation). If there is more than one owner, then the business is classified as a "General Partnership".

**PROS**:
- Easy to setup, easy to maintain.

**CONS**:
- Owners are **personally liable** for the company and its debt (the owner(s) could lose a house, cars, personal assets, etc.) in a lawsuit. Usually not recognized at the State level, only in your city/county. No corporate "prestige" of having the "Inc." or "LLC" attached to your name.

## Corporation

Many people do not know that there are two different types of corporation; a C Corporation and an S Corporation. The C Corporation is automatic when you submit your paperwork with the IRS. In order to become an S corporation, the corporation must submit a form signed by all the shareholders.

## C Corporation

A corporation is a separate legal entity that can shield the owners from personal liability and company debt. As a separate entity, it can buy real estate, enter into contracts, sue and be sued completely separately from its owners. Also, money can be raised easier via the sale of stock; its ownership can be transferred via the transfer of stock; the duration of the corporation is perpetual (the business can continue regardless of ownership); and the tax advantages can be considerable (i.e. you are able to deduct many business expenses, healthcare programs, etc. that other legal entities cannot). Income is reported completely separate via a tax return for the corporation.

A corporation is set up in the following structure:
- Shareholders own the stock of the corporation.
- Shareholders elect Directors (known as the "Board of Directors").
- Directors appoint Officers (President, Secretary, Treasurer, etc.).
- Officers run the company (day-to-day operations).

In many cases (especially during the startup phase), you will be the 100% owner of the stock, therefore you elect the directors (usually yourself), then appoint yourself as an officer.

The rules for operating your corporation are set in what are called Corporate Bylaws. This document sets the rules for the company and can be modified as the business grows and changes. Our Incorporation Service includes a fully personalized set of Corporate Bylaws for your State (as well as an editable copy) for you to modify as the company grows and changes.

Operating a corporation involves at the minimum holding a yearly Directors and Shareholders meeting (the location is determined by you and the expenses are deductible), keeping written minutes of major company decisions and maintaining general corporate compliance as dictated by the Corporate Bylaws.

**PROS:**
- The oldest, most successful and most prestigious type of business entity; provides personal liability protection; conveys permanence, can reduce taxes.
- Owners are protected from personal liability for company debts and obligations.
- Corporations have a reliable body of legal precedent to guide owners and managers.
- Corporations are the best vehicle for eventual public companies.
- Corporations can more easily raise capital and transfer ownership through the sale of securities.
- Corporations can have an unlimited life.
- Corporations can create tax benefits under certain circumstances, but note that C corporations may be subject to "double taxation" on profits. To avoid this, many business owners elect to operate their corporations under subchapter S of the Internal Code. Also known as an S corporation, this entity allows income to pass through to the individual shareholders.

**CONS:**
- More expensive to set up than a DBA; more paperwork and formality required than an LLC (holding Shareholder/Board meetings, keeping minutes and resolutions).
- Corporations require annual meetings and require owners and directors to observe certain formalities.
- Corporations are more expensive to set up than partnerships and sole proprietorships.
- Corporations require periodic filings with the state and annual fees.

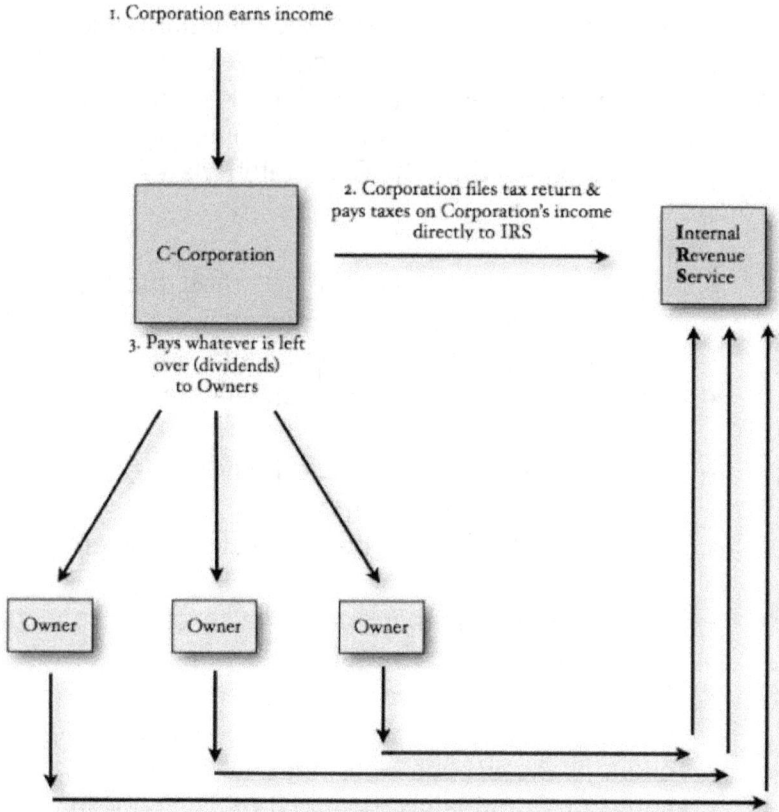

## S Corporation

After a corporation has been formed, it may elect "S Corporation Status" by adopting an appropriate resolution and completing and submitting a form to the Internal Revenue Service (some states require their own version). Once this filing is complete, the corporation is taxed like a partnership or sole proprietorship rather than a corporation. Thus, the income is "passed-through" to the shareholders for purposes of computing tax returns.

Most new small corporations elect S Corporation Status (90%+) so profits and losses can be added to the shareholders' personal tax returns without having to pay taxes on profits once, then again when they are given back to the shareholders as income (dividends). This is known as "double taxation" and is the reason why S Corporations were created. An S Corporation can also revert back to regular Corporation status fairly easily.

There are some limitations on S Corporations: they cannot deduct some expenses like health insurance, travel, entertainment, etc. that normal corporations can. Also, they are restricted to 100 shareholders or fewer and those shareholders must be U.S. Citizens. Finally, S Corporations may not own or be owned by other business entities.

**PROS:**
- Prestige of the corporation without the double taxation. Ideal for "1 person corporations".
- The key advantage of an S-Corp is that it offers tax benefits when it comes to excess profits, known as distributions. The S-Corp pays its employees a "reasonable" salary, which means it should be tied to industry norms, while also deducting payroll expenses like federal taxes and FICA. Then, any remaining profits from the company can be distributed to the owners as dividends, which are taxed at a lower rate than income.

**CONS:**
- More expensive to setup than a DBA; more paperwork and formality required than an LLC.
- S-Corps have stricter guidelines than LLCs. As per the tax code, you must meet the following standards to create an S Corporation:
    - Must be a U.S. citizen or resident.
    - Cannot have more than 100 shareholders.
    - Corporation can only have one class of stock.
    - Profits and losses must be distributed to the shareholders in proportion to the shareholder's interest.
- Shareholders must adhere to the requirements at all times.

- Passive income limitation: You can't have more than 25 percent of gross receipts from passive activities, such as real estate investment.
- There can be additional state taxes for S-Corps.
- Shareholders should pay attention to paying themselves a "reasonable" salary for the work they perform for the S-Corp, since the IRS is increasingly scrutinizing S Corporations for this.

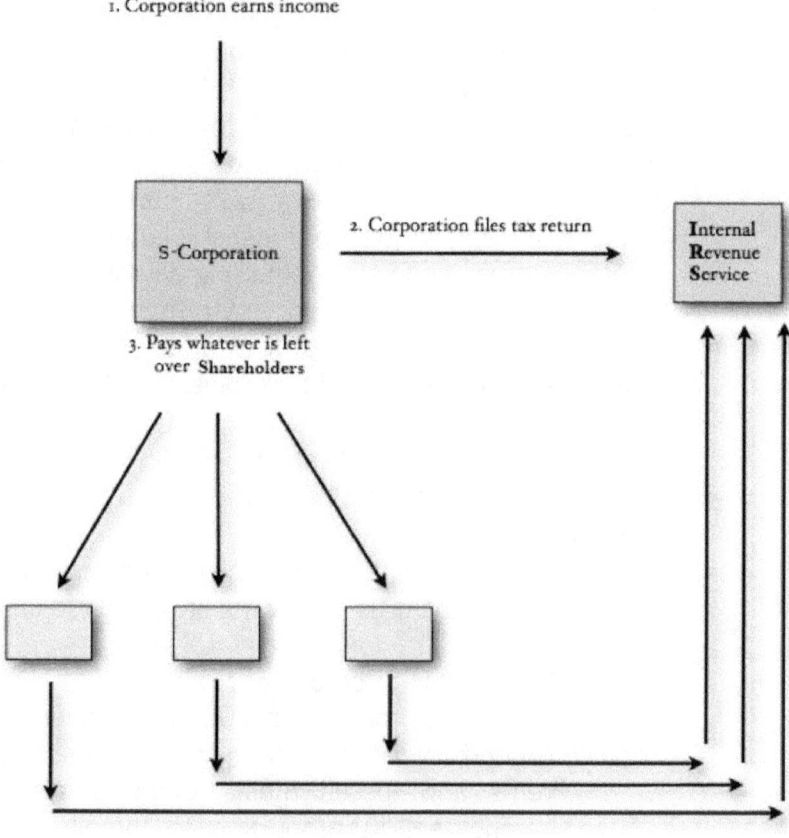

**Limited Liability Company**
A Limited Liability Company can be best described as a hybrid between a corporation and a partnership. It provides easy management and "pass-through" taxation like a Sole Proprietorship/Partnership, with the liability protection of a Corporation. It's a relatively new form of business, created in 1977 in Wyoming and now recognized in all 50 States and Washington D.C.

Like a corporation, it is a separate legal entity; unlike a corporation, there is no stock and there are fewer formalities. The owners of an LLC are called "Members" instead of "Shareholders". So in essence, it is like a corporation, but with less complicated taxation and stock formalities.

The heart of a Limited Liability Company is known as the "Operating Agreement". This document sets the rules for operating the company and can be modified as the business grows and changes.

Operating an LLC is less formal than a corporation, usually only requiring an Annual Members' Meeting and Members' agreeing to changes of the Operating Agreement and other major company decisions.

**PROS:**
- Provides the liability protection of a corporation without the corporate formalities (Board meetings, Shareholder meetings, minutes, etc.) and extra levels of management (Shareholders, Directors, Officers).
- The owner of a single member LLC doesn't have to file a tax return for the LLC, as they only report the activity on their personal tax return.
- Ease of setup: Most LLC forms are only a single page for single member LLCs.
- Inexpensive to start: The cost of setting up an LLC is also inexpensive, usually just a couple hundred dollars.

- Guidelines: The red tape involved in forming an LLC isn't as stringent as that involved with S corps, which also leads to savings on accountant and attorney fees, among others.

**CONS:**
- Usually more expensive to form than a DBA, requires more paperwork and formal behavior.
- Self-employment tax: Single member LLC owners are required to pay self-employment tax on income generated in the LLC, which means making quarterly estimated payments to the IRS.
- Owners of LLCs must make sure they don't pierce the "corporate veil," meaning they have to operate the LLC separately from their personal affairs.

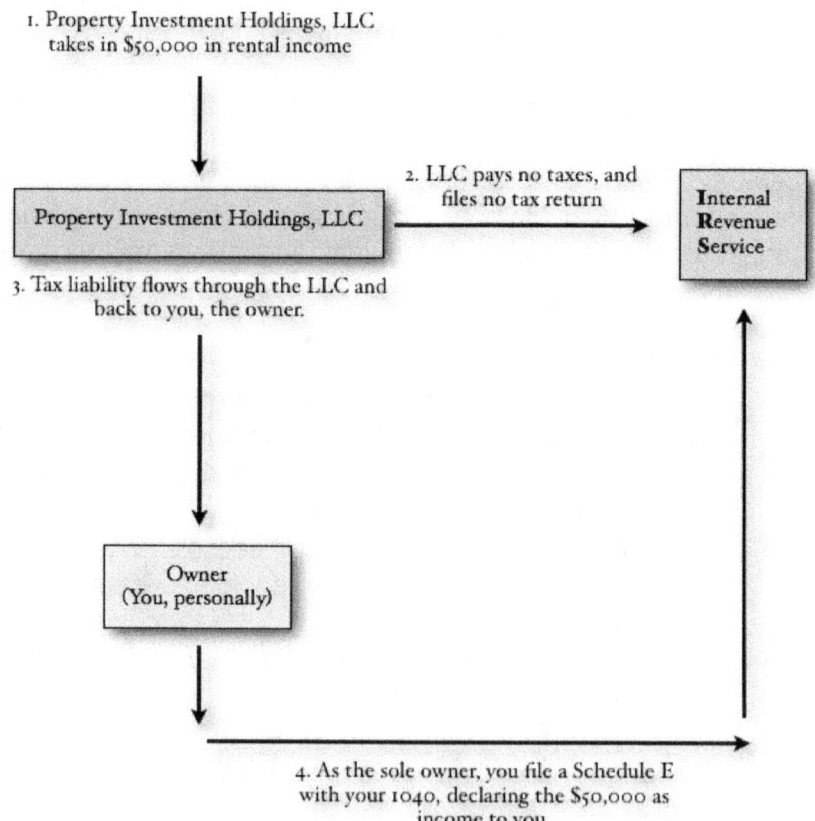

Take a look at our Business Comparison Matrix and it will give you, line by line, the difference between the entities.

| | S | P | LC | CC | SC |
|---|---|---|---|---|---|
| Owners have limited liability for business debts & obligations | | | X | X | X |
| Created by a state-level registration that usually protects the company name | | | X | X | X |
| Business duration can be perpetual | | | X | X | X |
| May have an unlimited # of owners | | X | X | X | |
| Owners need not be U.S. citizens or residents | X | X | X | X | |
| May be owned by another business, rather than individuals | | | X | X | |
| May issue shares of stock to attract investors | | | | X | X |
| Owners can report business profit and loss on their personal tax returns | X | X | X | | X |
| Owners can split profit & loss with the business for a lower overall tax rate | | | | X | |
| Permitted to distribute special allocations, under certain guidelines | | X | X | | |
| Not required to hold annual meetings or record meeting minutes | X | X | X | | |

S = Sole Proprietorship
P = Partnership
LC = Limited Liability Company
CC = C Type of Corporation
SC = S Type of Corporation

## *SPECIAL NOTE REGARDING ENTITIES:*

Here are the 5 Biggest Incorporation and LLC Creation Mistakes when it comes to business entities:

**Do-it-yourself.** - Filing the paperwork yourself and not doing the crucial after-formation tasks like adopting Corporate Bylaws or an LLC Operating Agreement by holding an Organizational Meeting. This includes issuing shares, properly capitalizing the company etc. and can lead to disastrous results in a lawsuit, partner dispute and even in getting funding or contracts.

**Choosing Delaware, Nevada or Wyoming without doing the research.** - Are there valid reasons for choosing these states? Yes. Should everyone choose these states? No. While this is a decision best left to a discussion with you and your "Power Team".

**Choosing the cheapest incorporation service (or the cheapest advertised price*).** If you could hear the horror stories of some of the messes we've had to clean up. Can you imagine if you used a "fly-by-night" company as your Registered Agent and they went out of business? What if you were served with a lawsuit and lost it by default because you saved a few bucks? A "$49" service often buries hidden fees in the state fee, charges outrageous fees for shipping or has massive hidden fees.

**Introductory (1-6 months free) and "Free" Registered Agent service.** - "Free" Registered Agent service in our experience has a nasty habit of becoming very expensive, rates start at "Free" and suddenly 18 months later you're paying $569/year - read the fine print.

**Not Doing Your Research.** The service looks great, the website looks professional, the fees are acceptable and you're ready to order. Have you verified their Better Business Bureau (BBB) Membership? Check to see if the company has been around for a while and if they've got verified testimonials or reviews.

## Which is the best business entity for Real Estate Investors?

In our professional option, while there are a few options available to you, the best structure for most people will be to form an LLC, or limited liability company. Why is the LLC such a good way to hold investment real estate? The short answer is that it gives the owners the same liability protection enjoyed through corporate ownership with all the federal tax advantages associated with the partnership. In the past 10 years, state legislatures have made LLCs easier to form and clarified the scope of liability protection enjoyed by the owners. At the same time, the IRS has simplified the process of achieving the desired single level of taxation.

The LLC is the almost perfect entity for holding investment real estate. An LLC is a hybrid, unincorporated entity created by state law. It is a cross between a corporation and a partnership specifically designed to provide the owners with three significant benefits:

- It has the limited-liability characteristics of a corporation.
- It is taxed like a partnership under federal tax law.
- It has the flexible structure of a partnership.

The primary advantage the LLC has compared to a corporation is how it is taxed. The primary advantage compared to a partnership is that the liability shield applies to all owners. Unlike the limited partnership, neither passive nor active owners have personal liability for the LLC's debts and obligations.

Why incorporate or form an LLC?
- Reduce Liability
- Add Credibility
- Build Business Credit
- Reduce Taxes
- Protect a 1-Person Company

Additionally, you can reduce your administrative costs by setting up a single "parent" LLC with many "sub LLCs" that own individual properties in certain states. The benefit arises in being able to have one LLC that is broken up into different component "cells" to isolate injuries from one property from spreading over to the other properties held within the separate cells. Each cell can have different members so this increases the flexibility by having different ventures with other investors within one Series LLC. Another distinguishing feature is that each cell will have its own name, contracts, accounts, and as of a private letter ruling published by the IRS in 2008, each series can have its own tax status. Thus, the Series LLC gives great flexibility of being able to create one LLC instead of multiple LLCs subject to multiple fees to the state where the Series LLC is created.

*HELP! I want to be a Real Estate Investor What Do I Do?*

## Who should I have on my "Power Team"?

Every good real estate investor should have a "power team" to help you through the transactions. This team should help you stay financially fit, adhere to legal transaction, and keep you from making mistakes. There are eight people that you should be in contact with during the real estate transactions:

- Realtor
- Mortgage Broker
- Banker
- Title Company
- Accountant
- Insurance Agent
- General Contractor
- Attorney

Additionally, you will need some other people to have in your back pocket when you need them. They include:

- Inspector
- Appraiser
- Landscaper
- Cleaner
- Electrician

Once you develop your power team you can start to think about the type of property and where it will be located.

# What is my first big decision?

There is some risk associated with investing in real estate, but if you are educated and careful, you can minimize that risk. The chart below shows the different types of real estate and the relative amount of risk associated with each. When considering investing in these different types of property it is important to understand the advantages and disadvantages of each type. In this section we will discuss each of these types of investments and what you need to know to make an educated decision when purchasing.

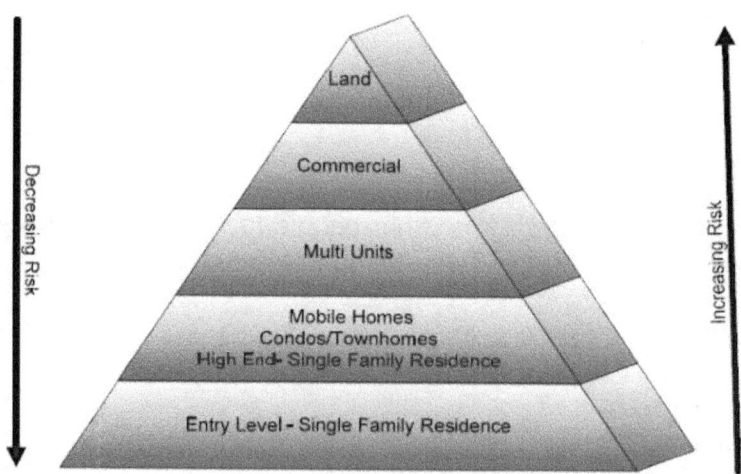

**Land** - Land has the highest risk of all the different types of real estate because it typically does not produce income and is slower to appreciate. You can buy land in one of two ways; either raw or improved.

> **Raw Land**— Raw land does not have utilities or amenities. It is land in its natural state, prior to grading, construction, and subdividing.

**Improved Land** — Improved land is the complete opposite; development is complete so all it needs is a building. If the land is accessible and usable the risk is much lower. In turn, the land holds a higher value.

**Commercial** - Real estate with the potential to generate outside income and/or revenue for the owner. Commercial property is another high risk property type. You will find that these properties require more money down and are harder to finance. What is considered commercial property? Strip malls, industrial parks, gas stations, convenience stores and office towers.

> The more profitable the property is, the more it is worth to investors.

Two great things about commercial real estate are that it generates income and appreciates over time. Most commercial properties are bought and held for a period of time.

Typically, the value of the property will increase or decrease with its ability to produce income. Your ability to attract tenants will dictate your ability to generate income for the property. Typically, if you are in a different state than the property, you will need a property management company or onsite manager to collect rents and maintain your property. As with any industry, you have both honest and dishonest people. In addition, property management expenses can become quite costly if they are not minimized and understood. You will want to keep a very close eye on the billed expenses.

**Multi-Unit** - Any property with two or more units that focuses on residential occupancy is considered a multi-unit. This can include many property types: Duplexes, 4-plexes, Apartment Complexes, etc.

> It is easier to acquire financing when the property has a positive cash flow already.

Multi-units are income generating properties, and have moderate risk compared to commercial properties. If your tenants pay for all of your expenses and you still have money left over each month, you have positive cash flow.

Negative cash flow means your monthly income is less than your monthly expenses, which means you have to take money out of your pocket to cover those monthly expenses.

**Mobile Homes** - Term used to describe factory-constructed homes installed on the home site. Trailer homes built before 1976 were often called mobile homes. Then, in 1976, the United States Congress passed the National Manufactured Housing Construction and Safety Act which assured that all homes were built to highly regulated standards, and they started calling them manufactured homes. For simplicity sake though, we will call them mobile homes. Mobile homes can have a mild risk level because of the minimal investment to purchase. They are also cheaper to repair.

**Condominiums/Townhomes** - Refers to any home that shares a building with other units. They generally have a mild risk level. Typically, a Home Owners Association (HOA) manages and maintains the building housing the condos and townhomes.

The more amenities that are available in the complex, the higher the value and desirability of the location. If the building is not well maintained, it can affect your property's value. Condos and town homes are more readily impacted by local and national market fluctuations. There is an exception to this rule however; in college and military towns these units can become very desirable and in many cases may be less risky to invest in than single family residences.

> If HOA increases the monthly fees too high or too often, your property may be harder to sell.

**Single family Residence** - Detached home, usually with a front and back yard, driveway, and attached carport or garage. When you are just getting started in investing in real estate, this is the ideal property type because the greatest portion of the population buys or rents this property type. Typically, it is the easiest property type to rent or sell because of the location, price and ease to qualify for financing. You will have a lot more buyers for this property type because these properties are attractive to first time home buyers, transitional home buyers, and other real estate investors.

Once you have identified the type of real estate in which you are going to invest, the next decision in identifying your personal property search criteria is, *"Where should I invest?"*

When choosing the location for a property it is important to understand the role of demographics. To evaluate the demographics of an area you would look at such things as:

- Crime rate
- Quality of schools
- Cost of living
- Proximity to hospitals, shopping, and transportation
- Tax rate
- Young families
- Retirees
- Singles
- Couples downsizing
- Other investors
- Detached dwelling
- Size of building (ft2)
- # of bedrooms and baths

Floor plan
- Attractive surroundings
- Moderately priced
- Steady appreciation
- Stable local economy
- Area's reputation
- Average # of days a property on market
- Medium to low property values
- Strong rental market
- Steady growth
- Lower tax rates

These are just a few of the things you need to be aware of for any property you want to look at. You want to find a location that has as many attractive demographic features as possible so that you don't limit who can buy or rent. The more potential buyers or renters you have the better. And the more attractive the demographics, the higher the price you can achieve for your investment.

# How do I find a property?

Now that you understand some of the characteristics of a good real estate investment the next question is; *where do you go to find it?* First let's look at some sources on the internet that you can use to find motivated sellers as well as learn more about your target areas. It is a two pronged approach, not only can you find out about your target area, but you can find motivated sellers too.

The sources mostly fall into one of these six categories:

- ➤ *On-line newspapers* - You can find the newspapers that are online by going to http://newslink.org or to an online search engine like Google and searching for "newspapers".

- ➤ *Free real estate services* - They are great places to learn about the market, find properties of interest, and even to sell your properties.

- ➤ *Real estate agent websites* - Buyers can access properties for sale for free on these websites.

- ➤ *Free newspapers* - These are the classified ad newspapers that you can pick up for free in gas stations, lube shops and grocery store entry ways. Most of them are region-specific and do not circulate nationwide.

- ➤ *Free on-line classifieds* - Internet search engines are database directories that house information and links to almost every website on the Internet.

- ➤ *Paid real estate listing services* - In addition to the free ones, there are a lot of paid real estate listing services online. They are another great source for properties with motivated sellers.

## *Special Note on Finding Houses:*

Here are the six worst ways to find houses:

1. Tracking down Condemned Houses (not vacant... Condemned Houses) These are too over shopped.

2. BANDIT SIGNS! Why? Most cities have really cracked down on these. Plus, homeowners have become much more active in picking them up.

3. What about expired listings? Again - over shopped. No top investor we know has successfully used this method.

4. Regular Newspaper Ads - For example... We Buy Houses 404-419-6524 - Why? Your ad does not stand out. It has something unique about it so that it stands out.

5. The Tax foreclosures are over shopped. They are good in outlying counties. They are also good if you plan to buy lots.

6. Flyers and business cards on bulletin boards. Why is this so bad? Too small time. If you want to get a lot of deals, you need to market on a much larger scale.

## Are there any pitfalls I should look out for?

The biggest mistake new investors make is they don't do their research on the county or the property. Doing it properly can lead to lots of profit, while ignoring this aspect of investing could cost you your investment. Perform all proper due diligence and you will eliminate the risk of over paying. Here are 5 tips to help you do your due diligence on properties and counties to ensure that you make a profitable investment!

### 1. Investors do not retrieve the public information about the property

Sometimes through the tax assessor's or the county clerk's website you can get information on the property. These records usually show all the information on the property used for valuation, type of property, assessed value, and sometimes you can even get the last sale data on the property. You may need to make a phone call to talk to someone to find out specific questions about the property.

### 2. A title search is not done BEFORE the purchase

Property records are public knowledge and can be found at the Register of Deeds office of the county where the property is located. Most counties also maintain online databases where property information may be obtained at no cost. It's always better to yield on the side of caution and get a professional one done. The cost of a professional doing the title search is worth the investment if you are very interested in specific property.

One of the reasons for doing a title search is to make sure that if you do find any lien holders. If the property owner, or any of the lien holders were not properly notified of the sale, they could contest the sale in court. You would get your money back, but you would have done all that work for nothing.

### 3. A physical review of the property is not done

A Geographic Information System (GIS) is a computer system designed to capture, store, manipulate, analyze, manage, and present all types of geographical data. It also shows if the property is in a flood plain, earthquake zone or other specific geographic areas. You can sometimes get a GIS map of the property from the property assessor's website.

Additionally, each state has an environmental website that list known environmental problems. Find the environmental website for the state that you are investing in and locate the list of known problem sites for the county. For a beginner we do not bid on any properties listed as known environmental problems. You may want to stay away from any properties that are near any of these problem sites.

### 4. Market value and neighborhood information is not determined

There are various websites that will give you comparisons of nearby properties and allow you to look up demographics about the area. Real Estate websites can give you estimates on what the value of the property would be, estimates on what properties around it would be and other neighborhood specific information.

### 5. A professional is not involved with the transaction

It always better to have a trusted advisor like a real estate agent to help with the specific about the property. A Real Estate Agent is a multifaceted individual, with duties that include buying, selling and renting properties for clients. They must have general real estate knowledge and know about the local markets in which they work. Their goal is to provide their clients with the best deals on properties that their companies possess while meeting the specific needs of clients. It addition you need a management team in the US to help you with the day to day operations of your real estate business.

# Is this property a good investment?

Qualifying a property is the process of research and evaluation you go through when deciding whether to make an offer to purchase it. There are two main factors to consider when you are qualifying a property. First, the price of the property has to meet your investment criteria. There are many formulas that investors use to determine if a deal meets their investment criteria. One formula investors use to determine their purchase price is the *fast offer formula*. The fast offer formula is used when you want to buy and sell properties quickly.

The formula is simple. Simply start with the average cost of the comparable properties after the repairs. Then subtract the costs of the transaction, the cost of repairing the property and the amount of profit you want to achieve. The result provides a good idea of what your maximum offer should be for the property.

> After Repair Value
> - Repair Costs
> - Purchase Costs
> - Holding Costs
> - Sales Costs
> - Minimum Profit (8 to 12%)
> - Overruns
> = **Maximum Purchase Price**

Real estate investing is all about the numbers. There are several points to consider when you are evaluating the numbers. If the numbers do not add up to a profit when you buy the property, you need to walk away from the deal. One number to consider is the purchase price, if that is not evaluated correctly you will lose money. Next, you need to consider the time frame to repair the property and costs to repair it. Then, since the property will be held for a certain period of time, you will need to know how much it will cost to hold onto it for that time. Finally, the most important number is how much profit is reasonable for a property in that area.

The second factor used to qualify properties is the property's condition. You will run into properties that don't have any economic life left in them, as well as properties that require very little fix-up. We recommended that you stick with properties that require no more than $10,000 to $12,000 in repairs. These costs will include new flooring and painting the property inside and out. One of the biggest mistakes a new investor makes is under estimating the cost of doing repairs and overestimating the after-repair value of a property. Be sure to get at least a couple of estimates on repair costs before making a decision on what you will offer for the property. Once you have reviewed the numbers it is time to purchase.

## Can I get the cash to purchase my real estate investment?

Money is typically one of the biggest concerns to a new real estate investor. Many people feel that even if they can secure good deals, they do not have the money to purchase them. Many of these people also do not know how to get the necessary financing so they let good, money-making properties pass them by. You are not going to be one of those people.

Let's quickly identify where you are right now in regards to finances. There are four main categories of personal finance:

1. **No down payment and bad credit**
2. **Down payment (Up to $5,000) and bad credit**
3. **Down payment of 5 % of the loan amount and good credit**
4. **Down payment of 10 to 20 % of the loan amount and good credit**

It may surprise you, but regardless of which of these categories best defines your situation, you can make money in real estate! So the question becomes: as an investor, do you need to worry about financing? And the answer is, NO. If you find a great deal, you can find the financing to make it happen.

### No down payment and bad credit
If you are in this category, don't worry. There are plenty of ways you can make money in Real Estate. Some of them include:
- Being a "Bird Dog" – You can find properties for other investors to purchase and collect a finder's fee.
- Assignment of Contract – To make this strategy work you need to get a property under contract at a wholesale price, then assign it, or transfer fulfillment of the contract to another investor for a fee.

- Participate in a Joint Venture – A person or group of people who have money to invest, and you enter into an agreement with them that they will supply the funds necessary for the purchase and possible repair of the property.
- Have seller financing - seller financing is when you have the seller or private investor act like the bank for you.
- Use a hard money lender - people or groups of people who lend money at traditionally higher rates than lending institutions and basically make their own rules when it comes to lending.

## Down payment (Up to $5,000) and bad credit

If you have a down payment up to $5,000 and bad credit, you have some additional options to choose from to start your real estate investing business. Additionally, the techniques available can be used if you have no down payment and bad credit, as described above.

- Lease Options - you lease the property with an agreement to buy it from the seller at a locked-in price at a later date.
- Sandwich Lease Options - Sandwich lease options are similar to traditional lease options but they differ in that you do not actually buy the property until your tenant is ready to buy from you.
- Small investor groups - The first is where everyone in the group is involved with everything. Everyone helps finance the property, everyone helps find it, fix it and sell it. The second option is where you select a group of members who are specialized in certain areas. For example, one member may have more money to contribute, someone else may have repair skills, and another may have marketing skills. This is a good option if you have a specific skill but not a lot of money.
- Seller Financing - A seller or private investor acts as a bank for you to secure the property.

## Down payment of 5 % of the loan amount and good credit
This option is for those investors that have more down payment but may not want the entire risk of the project in their hands.
- Small investor groups – The responsibilities and finances are shared between multiple people.
- Seller Financing – One individual finances the property with the knowledge that you are the title holder and they are the lending institution.

## Down payment of 10 - 20 % of the loan amount and good credit
If you have good credit and a good down payment, then the options are essentially limitless. You can even use the methods of purchasing described in the sections above to leverage your money. These may include:
- Traditional lending
- FHA
- VA

There are some other options that you may be eligible for if it is a good fit. You would want to talk to your real estate agent or someone in your "power team" to see if there are additional opportunities, such as tax lien certificates.

> Six Questions to ask your lender:
> - "Does the lender have any creative financing options for investors?"
> - "Does the lender have any no-money-down loans for investors?"
> - "Do you have any 5% or 10% down loans?"
> - "Do you have any "no documentation loans?"
> - "Does the lender allow the seller to carry the down payment and pay closing costs?"
> - "Will you lend based on the purchase price or the After Repair Value?"

# I have my property, now what?

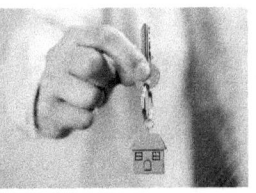

You should never purchase a property without having several investment strategies already in mind. You want several because conditions may change. For instance, you may be interested in doing a buy and sell, however, after buying the property you realize that the expected days-on market are six to nine months, so you need to switch to a buy and hold or a cash flow strategy. The shift in strategy may require some additional resources from you, but if you know your options you can make sure your deal is still profitable. It's important to be flexible and react quickly to preserve profit margins.

Another element of the numbers game is the number of properties available, the number of offers you make, and the number of deals that you do in a certain period of time. Keep in mind, the more offers you make, the more deals you will do, and the better your odds of earning a good income.

> A typical buyer looks at three to five houses before purchasing.

The typical investor looks at 10 to 20 properties before buying. However, the numbers could be higher depending on your area. It's important to remember that anyone can buy real estate for the asking price. Investors must purchase the property at a deep enough discount that when they sell it there is at least a 1% - 20% profit or at least $10,000. It takes significant resources and knowledge of the area to capture that amount of profit on every deal. We feel that $10,000 is a fair profit amount, but if you can make more all the better. Remember, your profit is determined when you purchase the property and not when you sell.

## How can I (legally) pay less taxes on my profits?

Congratulations on making money on your investment. A lot of hard work goes into it. Unfortunately, now that you have your profits, Uncle Sam needs their cut. Here are some ways you can legally reduce your capital gains on your property:

### 1. Limit the Rental Use of Your Home
If you choose to rent out your old house instead of selling it, you're in danger of losing the exclusion. To qualify for the exclusion, you must have lived in the home for two of the five years prior to the home sale. That means that the exclusion starts to phase out once you start to rent your house for three years, and you can potentially lose the exclusion completely. To avoid this situation and minimize your taxes, sell your one within three years of moving out or converting it to a rental.

### 2. Keep Records of Home Improvements
Keep thorough records of any home improvements or additions you've made to your home over the years. In addition to increasing your home's value, any improvements that you make to your home increase your basis in the home and thereby reduce your capital gain dollar for dollar. This tax-savings strategy can be particularly valuable if you have a gain because the property doesn't qualify for the primary residence exclusion, or you've exceeded your exclusion amount.

According to the IRS, an improvement is anything that betters your home, adapts it, or restores your home to a previous condition. Adding rooms, a deck, a pool, a retaining wall, or landscaping the property all count as improvements. Retain copies of receipts and records and keep a log of all the purchases you've made.

### 3. Track Selling Expenses

Capital gains are reduced by any expenses that you incur to sell the home. If you have a taxable capital gain because you've exceeded your exclusion or the property doesn't qualify, reporting these expenses will reduce your capital gain amount.

While you can't deduct cleaning or maintenance expenses from your reported selling price, there are many other selling costs that qualify. Nolo notes that settlement fees, broker commissions, escrow and closing costs, advertising and appraisal fees, points paid by the seller, title search fees, transfer taxes, and any miscellaneous document preparation fees can all reduce your capital gain. As with home improvements, keep records and receipts in case the IRS wants to see them.

### 4. Move Often

The IRS capital gain exclusion is large enough that many taxpayers will never have to pay taxes on the sale of their homes. However, if you've held your property for a long time, bought in a hot area, or are single, the exclusion may not completely cover your gain.

To use the capital gain exclusion to its fullest potential, you should consider a move when you've maxed out the capital gain exclusion on your home. Although you need to have lived in your house for at least two years to claim the exclusion, the IRS allows taxpayers to use the exclusion multiple times (no more than once every two years in general). This means you could potentially sell multiple homes at a large gain and never pay a dime in taxes.

### 5. Use a 1031 Exchange

Whenever you sell business or investment property and you have a gain, you generally have to pay tax on the gain at the time of sale. The tax-deferred exchange (also called tax free exchanges and 1031 exchanges) remains the most important tool in planning for non-personal real estate transactions.

The exchange can include like-kind property exclusively or it can include like-kind property along with cash, liabilities and property that are not like-kind. If you receive cash, relief from debt, or property that is not like-kind, however, you may trigger some taxable gain in the year of the exchange. There can be both deferred and recognized gain in the same transaction when a taxpayer exchanges for like-kind property of lesser value.

### Who qualifies for the Section 1031 exchange?
Owners consisting of individuals, C corporations, S corporations, partnerships (general or limited), limited liability companies, trusts, and any other taxpaying entity may set up an exchange of business or investment properties for business or investment properties under Section 1031.

### What can be exchanged?
To accomplish a Section 1031 exchange, there must be an exchange of properties. The simplest type of Section 1031 exchange is a simultaneous swap of one property for another.

### What can NOT be exchanged?
Personal residences and vacation homes (primarily personally used) do not qualify for tax-deferred exchanges. Real estate that is a property held primarily for sale (such as a home built for sale) can also NOT be exchanged.

Exchanges for partnership interests do not qualify for tax-deferral. If the real estate interest received is converted or contributed to a partnership shortly after the exchange, the transaction may be collapsed and the deferral disallowed.

### **What property qualifies for a Like-Kind Exchange?**

Both the relinquished property you sell and the replacement property you buy must meet certain requirements. There has been some discussion about curtailing the scope of real estate transactions qualifying for this treatment. For example, a motel would have to be exchanged for a motel; an apartment complex for an apartment complex, and so on.

Both properties must be held for use in a trade or business, or for investment. Property used primarily for personal use, like a primary residence or a second home or vacation home, does not qualify for like-kind exchange treatment. Both properties must be similar enough to qualify as "like-kind."

Like-kind property is property of the same nature, character or class. Quality or grade is not relevant. Most real estate will be like-kind to other real estate. Real property and personal property can both qualify as exchange properties under Section 1031; but real property can never be like-kind to personal property. In personal property exchanges, the rules pertaining to what qualifies as like-kind are more restrictive than the rules pertaining to real property.

This is a simplified explanation of some of the issues relating to tax-deferred exchanges. These are sensitive transactions, usually with high-stakes results. Taxpayers should be wary of individuals promoting use of like-kind exchanges. We highly recommend that you get professional help beyond a real estate agent to put a deal together. An investment in fees for legal and tax consulting help can pay off in avoiding unpleasant surprises later.

If you're considering a 1031 exchange here are 10 things you should know:
1. A 1031 isn't for personal use.
2. Some personal property qualifies.
3. "Like-kind" is broad.
4. You can do a "delayed" exchange.
5. You must designate a replacement property.
6. You can designate multiple replacement properties.
7. You must close within six months.
8. If you receive cash, it is taxable.
9. You must consider mortgages and other debt.
10. Using 1031 for a vacation house is tricky.

# What if I have losses on my real estate investment?

Although no one plans on having losses on a real estate investment but if you do there are some ways to use them to your advantage. If you actually lose out-of-pocket money on your investment property, the IRS treats your loss the same way as any other taxable loss. Therefore, you can use the following tricks to reduce your taxable income:

### Multiple Properties
When you own multiple properties, the IRS has you combine their individual profits and losses into a total income or loss from your rental property activities. Since you combine the properties, you can use a loss from one to offset another, thereby reducing your total taxable income. For example, if you make $18,000 on one rental property, but lose $6,000 on another, you'd end up with a total profit of $12,000, which would be part of your taxable income.

### Real Estate Professionals
When you're a real estate professional, your rental income and losses get treated as a part of your real estate enterprise, all of which is classed as active income. In this instance, your rental losses can be applied to reduce your taxable income on a dollar-for-dollar basis. You need to pass three tests to be considered a real estate professional by the IRS, though. You need to spend at least half of your productive time in the practice of real estate. The time you spend doing real estate must be at least 750 hours per year. Finally, you can't be an employee anywhere other than at a real estate-related company of which you own 5 percent or more.

## Passive Activity Losses

If you aren't a real estate professional, you can write off up to $25,000 of your rental property losses, called passive activity losses by the IRS, against other income. To qualify for this write-off, you need to be actively involved in running your rental properties, although you can have a third-party manager helping you. You also need to have an Adjusted Gross Income that is $100,000 or less. Your ability to claim the passive activity loss deduction starts going down by $1 for every $2 of income that you have over the $100,000 threshold. If your AGI is $150,000 or more, you won't be able to claim any losses.

## Carryforwards

Any rental property losses that you have left after your passive activity loss deduction, if any, don't go away. You get to save them up for use in a future year. The IRS lets you carry forward any passive activity losses to offset other passive income. For example, if you have $5,000 in unused losses this year and a $9,000 profit next year, you'll be able to use the losses to turn the $9,000 profit into a $4,000 taxable profit. You can even deduct this year's losses in the future if your income goes down so that you're eligible to claim them.

# Are there tax incentives for Real Estate Investments?

The effectiveness in protecting income from taxation is the true test of any real estate corporation. Most real estate is purchased, at least in part, because of the tax benefits that the shareholders can accrue. Ownership of real estate can produce substantial tax savings that can transform a fair investment into a very good one. The goal is to protect large amounts of income – accruing from the property itself or from other sources – from taxation. Investment real estate can be very effective at doing this. Deductions that are available for most real estate investments include the following:

- Mortgage loan interest can be deducted to offset an equal amount of income. Borrowing $50,000 at 9% interest will yield an interest deduction of $4,500 during the first year of the loan, which can be used to offset $4,500 of income that would ordinarily be subject to income tax. Regarding its effect on taxes, the interest deduction for investment real estate is the same as the interest deduction for a home mortgage.

- Property taxes levied against investment real estate and paid to state or local governments can also be deducted from taxable income. The deduction for property taxes you pay on investment real estate is treated in the same manner as the property taxes paid on your home, if you itemize deductions. The higher the property taxes you pay, the greater the tax savings you can achieve.

- Insurance premiums for coverage of real estate investments are deductible from taxable income. Insurance premiums are not deductible for homeowners.

- Maintenance expenses are fully deductible in calculating the tax liability for a real estate investment. Expenses you incur for repairing rotting wood around the water heater or painting the deck are examples of costs that can be deducted from your other income, thus arriving at a lower tax bill. Maintenance costs can be quite substantial, especially for older properties (or properties that might be rented to college students, for example). Being able to deduct those expenses is a very important benefit of owning investment real estate, one which is not available to homeowners.

- Improvements that prolong the life or increase the value of the real estate are treated differently from maintenance costs, however. While maintenance expenses can be deducted in the year that they're incurred, improvement costs must be used to increase the cost basis of the real estate, thereby reducing any gain or increasing any loss when the property is eventually sold.

- Depreciation accounts for the decline in value of an asset over time, including most real estate. Depreciation decreases the accounting value (the value of the property as shown on financial statements) of real estate and at the same time offsets an equal amount of income from taxation, yet does not affect the market value of the property. Investors generally obtain maximum tax benefits by depreciating real estate as quickly as possible. Rapid depreciation offsets income and saves taxes sooner. Residential rental property currently must be depreciated equally over twenty-seven and one-half years, while commercial investment property must be depreciated over thirty-nine years.

- The maximum Capital Gains Federal Tax Rate on capital gains is 15%, whereas wage income is taxed at 35%. There's state taxes, too, and some states offer further discounts on capital gains income. Remember, capital gains require that you hold a property for 12 months or more before selling and that it was held for productive use (i.e., as a rental, not a long-term fix and flip).

- You can get an Exemption for Principal Residence if you sell your residence; the first $250,000 is exempt from gain or

$500,000 if you are married. Remember, this requires that the residence was used as such for two of the last five years.

- Under Internal Revenue Code Sec 1031, you can roll your profits from a rental property into more real estate and defer paying taxes altogether. Your tax basis rolls into the next property.

> Here are the top five tax tips for Real Estate Investors:
> 1. Get a good accountant
> 2. Hold short term & long term investments in different entities
> 3. Get organized
> 4. Own rental property
> 5. Earn income like the wealthy

## About the Authors

### Vidal Espinosa

Vidal Espinosa, MBA has more than 20 year of accounting experience. Working for large accounting firms such as KPMG and Deloitte. During his time at KPMG, he provided tax advice to various corporations including being an external CFO for various multinational companies like Sushi ITTO and Sanyo.

He is a Certified Public Accountant in Mexico from the Universidad Pan Americana in Mexico City and Cetys Universidad in Tijuana and holds a Master's Degree in International Business by Universidad Iberoamericana and Business Management by IPADE Business School in Mexico. As a former professor at Loyola University, he focused on resolving and analyzing competitive problems related to the International Markets for Small and Medium Companies.

Currently Vidal is very involved with the local business community. He co-founded Invictus Advisors Foundation a non-profit 501 (c) 3 he is on the Advisory Board of the Hispanic Chamber of E-Commerce and Co-Founder of the Hispanic Chamber of E-Commerce Foundation.

His most recent accomplishments include: 2016 San Diego Latino Champion Business Leader of the Year presented by the San Diego Union Tribune and SDG&E; San Diego Best Accounting Firm in 2016 from the San Diego Union Tribune Readers Poll; Finalist as the CFO of the Year Awards 2016 by San Diego Business Journal; Top Minority Owned Business 2016 by San Diego Business Journal; Nominee for Latino Impact Awards by San Diego Magazine; and the best accountant in Mission Valley according to Yelp.

His Amazon Best Selling Book "HELP! The IRS is after me. What do I do?" provides individuals concreate steps and specific situations that can be used to help get the IRS off of your back.

## Arturo Soler

Arturo Soler has been a licensed real estate agent in California practicing real estate for over 10 years and has overseen over 75 million dollars in real estate transactions. Arturo has a Bachelor of Business Administration from Franco Mexicano de Monterrey and a Law Degree from Universidad Autonoma de Baja California.

As one of the top 2% producers in the nation and a 5-star agent, according to Zillow, Arturo is well versed on the entire real estate transaction. As one of very few agents that has received a Five Star Best Agent from San Diego Magazine (for two years in row) he understands the needs of his clients and gives them the best value for their dollar. HomeLight, a platform to use data and agent reviews to connect home buyers and sellers with the best real estate agents in their area, ranks Arturo as one of the top 1% of agents in Chula Vista for successfully selling homes and selling them fast.

Arturo has been interviewed by CNN iReport, the New York Times, Dream Home Magazine, ESPN 1700 AM Radio and countless others. He has been featured in many publications including: Coronado Eagle, San Diego Union Tribune, Robb Report, San Diego Magazine, Group Expansion, and Quien Magazine.

His professional memberships include: The California Association of Realtors, San Diego Association of Realtors, La Jolla Association of Realtors and many others.

Vidal Espinosa, MBA and Arturo Soler

## About Invictus Advisors

In the accounting, tax and business consulting field there seems to be a way to make it to the top and become a forefront industry specialist. Invictus Advisors has done that, in San Diego, California and beyond. Countless clients in various industries turn to us for a host of special services, and their record of delivery has surpassed many of our competitors. Bilingual service is yet another advantage securing them as a proactive problem-solving team of professionals.

Invictus works with clients and places a strong emphasis on relationships. We have come up with so many solutions that free up client time, something known as task time reduction. Essentially, our savvy becomes that of the clients; because our heart is for our clients. Our desire is to see them grow, thrive and become optimally successful in their chosen industry.

The wide array of skills that the partners have picked up is of particular pride. They are equipped to help small and large businesses to meet their organizational goals and legal obligations. Some things are inescapable, such as taxes. Organizations without internal personnel to handle this are flocking to Invictus for help.

Contact information:
Invictus Advisors
2815 Camino del Rio S Ste 250
San Diego CA 92108
619-677-6512
www.invictus-advisors.com

## About ARSO Real Estate Premier

ARSO Real Estate Premier is your ultimate resource for the latest property listings as well as community information, real estate guides and tools, and updates on the housing market in the region. Offering a personalized bilingual service that is both confidential and professional, in a trustworthy business environment, ARSO Real Estate has become the premier San Diego real estate company.

Wanting your home-buying or selling experience to be as easy and straightforward as it can be ARSO Real Estate Premier wants to earn your trust. They are not just in the business of processing transactions, they foster long-term relationships and to help their clients discover for themselves what a wonderful place to live San Diego truly is.

Their team is about getting you the best value for your investment and ensuring that the entire home-buying process will be as smooth and stress-free as it can possibly be. Whether it is a listing or sale, ARSO Real Estate will do it's best to deliver.

To top it all off they have dedicated websites to all the Luxury home markets in south San Diego including: Coronado, Eastlake, Rolling Hills, and Otay Ranch.

Contact information:
ARSO Real Estate Premier
333 W. Harbor Drive
San Diego, CA 92101
619-271-9152
www.arsorealestate.com

www.ingramcontent.com/pod-product-compliance
Lightning Source LLC
Chambersburg PA
CBHW070404190526
45169CB00003B/1103